Vampires in Nature

BY KIRSTEN W. LARSON

AMICUS HIGH INTEREST ✦ AMICUS INK

Table of Contents

What Are Vampires?

It wants to suck your blood. In the dark of night, it swoops in. It bites your neck. Slurp. It swallows your blood. Then it flies off, looking for its next **victim**. Scary! Is it a vampire? Yes. But it is not the type you read about in stories. It is a mosquito. And it is one of many bloodsucking animals.

Mosquitos want to suck your blood. They use a tube-like mouth to drink blood.

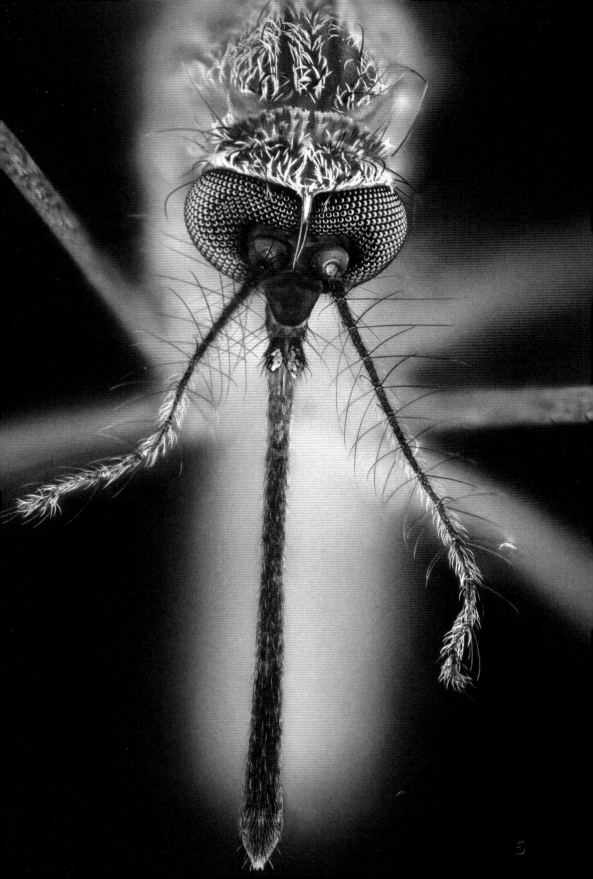

You've probably been bitten by a mosquito before. They leave itchy bites!

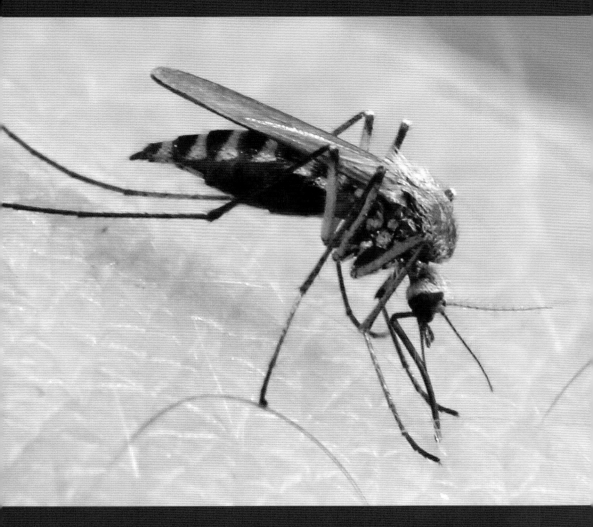

 Are all mosquitos bloodsuckers?

Bloodsuckers of the Sky

The vampires in stories have many different ways to find their victims. But a mosquito senses heat and movement. It detects the air you breathe out. It lands on your arm. Then it stabs with two needle-like tubes. One stops blood from **clotting**. The other sucks up blood. Gulp!

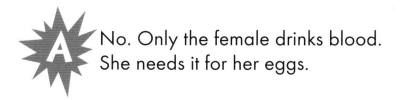
No. Only the female drinks blood. She needs it for her eggs.

On the Galapagos Islands, the vampire finch eats seeds and **nectar**. Sometimes, this food is hard to find. So the finch has an unusual **adaptation**. It also sips blood from other kinds of birds. Using its sharp beak, the finch pecks a small hole near the bird's wing. Then it laps up the blood. The pecking can harm baby birds. But it just annoys adults.

The vampire finch drinks blood when it doesn't find other food.

The vampire bat can smell an animal's blood. Then it goes in for the attack!

 How much blood does the bat eat?

A vampire bat soars through the darkened rainforest. It is out for blood. That is all it eats. But it's not looking for human blood. It prefers cows or wild animals. When it finds an animal, it crawls on the ground to the animal's ankle. Then it slits the skin with knife-like teeth. Using its tongue, it laps up the red liquid.

 It eats half its body weight. And it pees while it eats. That makes room for more food.

Water Vampires

The eel-like sea lamprey feasts on fish blood. It grabs fish with its circular rows of teeth. Using its sharp tongue, it makes a hole. Then it sucks blood like a vacuum. Lampreys live in the Atlantic Ocean and the Great Lakes. There they sip from trout, salmon, and even sharks. This often kills the fish.

There are up to 12 rows of teeth that grab onto prey inside a lamprey's mouth.

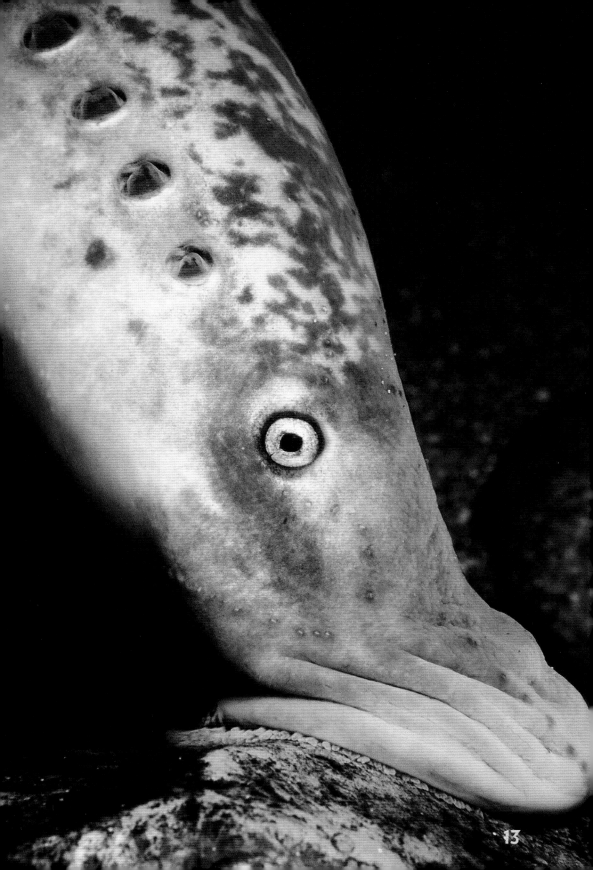

The small vampire catfish is also called a candiru. The largest are 16 inches (41 cm) long.

 Q Do vampire catfish bite people?

The Amazon River is known for killer fish like piranhas. But it is also home to the vampire catfish. This fish slips under the flaps covering another fish's **gills**. It hooks itself in place with **spines** around its head. It bites down. The blood flows. The fish feeds for a minute or more. Then it swims away.

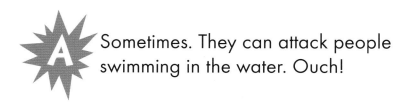 Sometimes. They can attack people swimming in the water. Ouch!

Leeches cling to reeds in the swamp. They are waiting for their next meal. Sensors on their skin tell them if a fish is near. The leeches dart toward the feast. Dinnertime! They chomp down with hundreds of teeth. Then they gulp several times their body weight in blood.

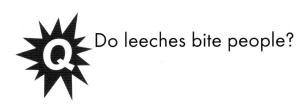 Do leeches bite people?

Leeches come in different sizes.
Some are small, like this one.

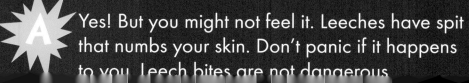

Yes! But you might not feel it. Leeches have spit
that numbs your skin. Don't panic if it happens
to you. Leech bites are not dangerous.

Lice can be hard to spot in a person's hair. Even the adults are smaller than a grain of rice.

 Q Will I get head lice?

Creepy Crawling Vampires

Scratch. Scratch. An itchy head is one clue that a vampire was here. Head lice suck only human blood. They stick near the scalp to stay warm. There they drink several times a day. Lice can live for about a month. But without their food, they would only live a day or two.

Maybe! Lice are common and spread easily. Don't share things that touch your head or hair. Use only your own combs, brushes, or hats.

You may have picked up a tick playing in the backyard. They climb to the tip of a leaf. They wave two legs in the air. Then they catch your clothes or hair. Then hooks on their feeding tubes lock their heads beneath your skin. They suck up your blood. If you find a tick on you, ask an adult to help you get it off. Some ticks can spread **Lyme disease**.

This deer tick is only 0.14 inch (3.5 mm) long.

Tiny hairs on the legs of fleas help them move around in cat fur.

 Are fleas deadly?

Do you have dogs or cats? Then your house may have fleas. Fleas have hairs on their legs that help them climb through hair. They also hop from animal to animal. Once on board, they use their needle-like tubes to slurp blood. Fleas do not normally live on people. But you could get a bite when petting your dog.

 They can be. During the Middle Ages, rat fleas helped spread the plague. Half the people in Europe died from this sickness.

You may have heard the phrase, "Sleep tight. Don't let the bedbugs bite." Bedbugs are unwanted sleepover guests. These insects are about the size of an apple seed. They hide in some people's mattresses. When you sleep, they climb over for a midnight snack. Their bites usually don't hurt. But they are itchy. After sucking your blood for about 10 minutes, the bedbugs dart back to their hideout.

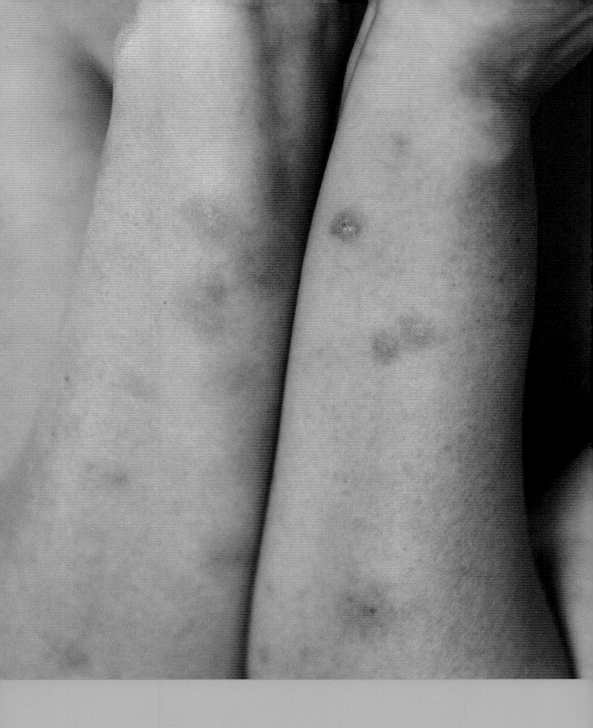

The red marks on this woman's arms are from bedbug bites.

A kissing bug's "kiss" is really a bite. These nighttime visitors bite near people's mouths or eyes. They spread a dangerous disease. The bugs poop when they eat. And that poop carries a **parasite**. If it enters the body through the bug bite, the person gets sick. Yikes! But don't worry too much. These bugs mostly live in Central and South America.

This kissing bug cousin is found in Europe.

Vampire Villains?

These vampires in nature seem like bad guys. But unlike vampires in stories, most of these animals do not kill. They just sip a little blood. But these "vampire" bites can spread diseases. First, the animal bites a person who is already sick. When it bites again, the next person might get sick, too. It's best to avoid these vampires!

A tick waits in the grass for its next victim. Watch out for this vampire!

Glossary

adaptation A change in a living thing that makes it better able to live in their environment.

clotting Sticking together and becoming thicker.

gills The parts of a fish on each side of its mouth that allow it to breathe.

Lyme disease A sickness that can cause fever, headaches, and a rash; it is spread by tick bites.

nectar A sweet liquid found in flowers.

parasite A creature that lives on or in another animal to survive.

spines Sharp spikes.

victim A creature that is hurt or killed by another.